EMMANUEL JOSEPH

Eco-Chic, The Intersection of Style, Sustainability, and Moral Responsibility

Copyright © 2025 by Emmanuel Joseph

All rights reserved. No part of this publication may be reproduced, stored or transmitted in any form or by any means, electronic, mechanical, photocopying, recording, scanning, or otherwise without written permission from the publisher. It is illegal to copy this book, post it to a website, or distribute it by any other means without permission.

First edition

This book was professionally typeset on Reedsy.
Find out more at reedsy.com

Contents

1	Chapter 1: The Fashion Paradox	1
2	Chapter 2: Sustainable Fabrics	3
3	Chapter 3: The Rise of Ethical Fashion Brands	5
4	Chapter 4: Vintage and Secondhand Fashion	7
5	Chapter 5: The Capsule Wardrobe Concept	9
6	Chapter 6: The Power of Upcycling	11
7	Chapter 7: Responsible Consumption	13
8	Chapter 8: The Impact of Fast Fashion	15
9	Chapter 9: Sustainable Fashion Events	17
10	Chapter 10: The Role of Technology in Sustainable Fashion	19
11	Chapter 11: The Intersection of Culture and Sustainability	21
12	Chapter 12: Fashion and Climate Change	23
13	Chapter 13: Circular Fashion Economy	25
14	Chapter 14: Fashion and Social Justice	27
15	Chapter 15: The Future of Sustainable Fashion	29
16	Chapter 16: The Role of Education in Sustainable Fashion	31
17	Chapter 17: A Call to Action	33

1

Chapter 1: The Fashion Paradox

Fashion has always been about expression, identity, and culture. Yet, it is paradoxically one of the most environmentally damaging industries in the world. The journey of clothing from the catwalk to landfill underscores the deep flaws in the fashion system. This chapter unravels how the paradox of fashion as both an art form and a source of environmental degradation came into existence. Historical contexts, such as the Industrial Revolution, set the stage for mass production, leading to fast fashion. As consumers, we must question our complicity in this cycle of consumption and waste.

The cost of cheap, disposable fashion is steep, not just for our wallets but for the planet. The exploitation of natural resources, energy-intensive production processes, and harmful pollutants from dyeing and finishing textiles contribute to a significant carbon footprint. However, fashion isn't solely to blame. Our relentless pursuit of new trends, fueled by a culture of disposability, exacerbates the problem. This chapter explores how our consumption patterns drive the demand for fast fashion and its repercussions on the environment.

Ethical considerations are also central to the fashion paradox. The working conditions in sweatshops, where many of our clothes are made, reveal a darker side of the industry. Workers, often women and children, are subjected to unsafe environments and meager wages. The fashion industry's moral responsibility extends beyond sustainability to ensuring fair labor practices. By understanding these interconnected issues, we can begin to envision a more responsible and sustainable fashion future.

Sustainability in fashion is no longer a niche concern but a pressing imperative. Designers, brands, and consumers are increasingly recognizing the need for change. Innovations in sustainable materials, circular fashion, and transparent supply chains offer hope for a greener industry. This chapter concludes by highlighting the role of conscious consumerism in driving this transformation. By making informed choices, we can support brands that prioritize the planet and people, not just profit.

Chapter 2: Sustainable Fabrics

The foundation of eco-chic fashion lies in the choice of materials. Traditional fabrics like cotton and polyester have significant environmental impacts, from water-intensive cultivation to non-biodegradable waste. This chapter delves into the world of sustainable fabrics, exploring alternatives that minimize harm and maximize style. Organic cotton, hemp, and bamboo are just a few examples of eco-friendly textiles that are gaining popularity. These materials offer a blend of comfort, durability, and environmental benefits.

Organic cotton is grown without harmful pesticides and synthetic fertilizers, reducing its ecological footprint. Hemp, often dubbed the "miracle plant," requires minimal water and no pesticides, making it an ideal sustainable fabric. Bamboo, too, is a fast-growing plant that regenerates quickly and requires less water compared to conventional crops. These fabrics represent a shift towards more sustainable agricultural practices and reduced resource consumption.

Innovations in fabric technology are also driving sustainability in fashion. Recycled materials, such as polyester made from plastic bottles, are transforming waste into wearable fashion. Similarly, biodegradable fabrics, like Tencel and Piñatex, offer eco-friendly alternatives to traditional textiles. Tencel, derived from wood pulp, is not only biodegradable but also requires less energy and water to produce. Piñatex, made from pineapple leaf fibers, is an innovative substitute for leather, offering a cruelty-free option for eco-conscious consumers.

Choosing sustainable fabrics is just one part of the equation. This chapter also explores the importance of responsible manufacturing processes. Ethical production practices, such as reducing water and energy usage, minimizing waste, and ensuring fair labor conditions, are integral to sustainable fashion. By supporting brands that prioritize these principles, consumers can contribute to a more ethical and environmentally friendly fashion industry.

3

Chapter 3: The Rise of Ethical Fashion Brands

As awareness of fashion's environmental and ethical impacts grows, a new wave of brands is emerging to challenge the status quo. These ethical fashion brands prioritize sustainability, transparency, and social responsibility. This chapter profiles some of the pioneers in the industry, from established names to up-and-coming designers. By highlighting their innovative approaches and commitment to ethical practices, we can inspire a shift towards more responsible fashion consumption.

Patagonia, a trailblazer in sustainable fashion, has long been committed to environmental responsibility. The brand's dedication to using recycled materials, reducing waste, and supporting fair labor practices sets a high standard for the industry. Similarly, Stella McCartney's eponymous label is renowned for its cruelty-free approach to luxury fashion, eschewing leather and fur in favor of sustainable alternatives.

Emerging brands like Reformation and Everlane are also making waves with their transparent business models and eco-friendly practices. Reformation focuses on sustainable fabrics, ethical manufacturing, and minimal waste, while Everlane champions radical transparency by revealing the true cost of their products and the factories they work with. These brands are redefining what it means to be fashionable by prioritizing the planet and people over profit.

Supporting ethical fashion brands is not just about making a statement; it's about making a difference. By choosing to invest in companies that prioritize sustainability and social responsibility, consumers can drive change in the industry. This chapter concludes by emphasizing the power of conscious consumerism and the collective impact of our choices. Together, we can create a fashion landscape that is both stylish and sustainable.

4

Chapter 4: Vintage and Secondhand Fashion

One of the most sustainable ways to indulge in fashion is through vintage and secondhand clothing. This chapter explores the allure of pre-loved fashion, from the thrill of discovering unique pieces to the environmental benefits of extending the life of garments. By choosing vintage and secondhand clothing, consumers can reduce waste and minimize their carbon footprint while embracing a timeless sense of style.

Vintage fashion is a celebration of history and individuality. Each piece tells a story, reflecting the styles and trends of bygone eras. The charm of vintage clothing lies in its uniqueness and the sense of connection it provides to the past. By wearing vintage, fashion enthusiasts can express their individuality while contributing to a more sustainable fashion ecosystem. This chapter delves into the cultural significance of vintage fashion and its role in promoting a circular economy.

Secondhand shopping has become increasingly popular, thanks to the rise of thrift stores, online marketplaces, and clothing swap events. This chapter explores the various avenues for finding pre-loved fashion, from local thrift shops to online platforms like Depop and ThredUp. By embracing secondhand fashion, consumers can save money, reduce waste, and support a more sustainable and ethical fashion industry.

The environmental benefits of vintage and secondhand fashion are significant. By extending the life of garments, we can reduce the demand for new clothing production and minimize the associated environmental impacts. Additionally, secondhand shopping encourages a more mindful approach to consumption, fostering a culture of reuse and recycling. This chapter concludes by highlighting the role of vintage and secondhand fashion in promoting sustainability and celebrating individuality.

5

Chapter 5: The Capsule Wardrobe Concept

A capsule wardrobe is a carefully curated collection of timeless, versatile pieces that can be mixed and matched to create a variety of outfits. This chapter explores the benefits of adopting a capsule wardrobe, from reducing clutter to minimizing environmental impact. By focusing on quality over quantity, we can embrace a more sustainable and stylish approach to fashion.

The concept of a capsule wardrobe dates back to the 1970s, when boutique owner Susie Faux introduced the idea as a solution to the fast-paced fashion cycle. A capsule wardrobe consists of essential items, such as a classic white shirt, a tailored blazer, and a pair of well-fitting jeans. These pieces are designed to be durable, timeless, and versatile, allowing for endless outfit combinations. By investing in high-quality, timeless garments, we can reduce the need for frequent shopping and the associated environmental impact.

Building a capsule wardrobe requires thoughtful consideration of personal style and lifestyle needs. This chapter provides practical tips for creating a capsule wardrobe, including assessing existing clothing, identifying gaps, and selecting versatile pieces. The goal is to create a cohesive collection that reflects individual style while minimizing waste and promoting sustainability.

Adopting a capsule wardrobe mindset encourages mindful consumption and a focus on quality over quantity. By prioritizing timeless pieces and versatile basics, we can reduce the environmental impact of our fashion choices. This chapter concludes by highlighting the benefits of a capsule wardrobe, from simplifying daily dressing to supporting a more sustainable fashion industry.

6

Chapter 6: The Power of Upcycling

Upcycling is the process of transforming old, worn-out, or discarded items into new, useful products. This chapter delves into the creative world of upcycling fashion, from DIY projects to designer collections. By breathing new life into old garments, we can reduce waste, conserve resources, and embrace a unique, personalized style.

Upcycling offers endless possibilities for creativity and self-expression. Old jeans can be transformed into stylish shorts, a vintage scarf can become a chic handbag, and a worn-out t-shirt can be repurposed into a trendy tote bag. This chapter provides inspiration and practical tips for upcycling fashion, encouraging readers to experiment with their own DIY projects.

Designers and brands are also embracing the upcycling movement. Pioneers like Christopher Raeburn and Marine Serre are known for their innovative upcycled collections, showcasing the potential of repurposed materials in high fashion. By incorporating upcycled elements into their designs, these creatives are challenging the traditional fashion system and promoting sustainability.

Upcycling not only reduces waste but also encourages a more thoughtful approach to consumption. By valuing and repurposing what we already have, we can minimize our environmental impact and contribute to a more sustainable fashion ecosystem. This chapter concludes by celebrating the transformative power of upcycling and its role in shaping a more sustainable fashion future.

7

Chapter 7: Responsible Consumption

Responsible consumption is about making informed choices that prioritize sustainability and ethical considerations. This chapter explores the principles of responsible consumption, from understanding the environmental and social impacts of our purchases to supporting brands that align with our values. By adopting a more mindful approach to fashion, we can reduce our carbon footprint and promote a more ethical industry.

One of the key principles of responsible consumption is transparency. Consumers have the right to know where and how their clothes are made, including the environmental and social impacts of the production process. This chapter highlights the importance of transparency in the fashion industry and provides tips for identifying brands that prioritize ethical practices.

Another aspect of responsible consumption is supporting local and independent designers. By choosing to invest in small businesses and artisans, we can promote more sustainable and ethical fashion practices. This chapter profiles some of the talented designers who are making a positive impact in the industry, from slow fashion pioneers to innovative eco-friendly brands.

Responsible consumption also involves reducing waste and embracing a more minimalist mindset. This chapter provides practical tips for curating a more sustainable wardrobe, including shopping less, choosing quality over quantity, and caring for clothes to extend their lifespan. By making conscious choices, we can contribute to a more sustainable and ethical fashion industry.

8

Chapter 8: The Impact of Fast Fashion

Fast fashion is characterized by its rapid production cycles, low prices, and disposable nature. This chapter examines the environmental and social impacts of fast fashion, from resource depletion to labor exploitation. By understanding the true cost of fast fashion, we can make more informed and responsible choices.

The environmental impact of fast fashion is significant. The industry is one of the largest consumers of water and energy, and the production process releases harmful pollutants into the air and water. This chapter explores the various environmental consequences of fast fashion, including deforestation, water pollution, and carbon emissions. By highlighting these issues, we can raise awareness and encourage more sustainable practices.

The social impact of fast fashion is equally concerning. The demand for cheap, disposable clothing has led to the exploitation of workers in developing countries. Many garment workers are subjected to unsafe working conditions, long hours, and low wages. This chapter delves into the human cost of fast fashion and emphasizes the importance of supporting brands that prioritize fair labor practices.

The culture of disposability promoted by fast fashion also contributes to significant waste. The average person discards a large amount of clothing each year, much of which ends up in landfills. This chapter examines the waste generated by fast fashion and offers solutions for reducing our impact, such as recycling, donating, and embracing secondhand shopping.

9

Chapter 9: Sustainable Fashion Events

Sustainable fashion events are gaining momentum as platforms for promoting eco-friendly practices and raising awareness about the environmental impact of the fashion industry. This chapter explores the rise of sustainable fashion events, from eco-friendly fashion weeks to zero-waste fashion shows. By showcasing innovative designs and sustainable practices, these events inspire change and highlight the importance of responsible fashion.

Eco-friendly fashion weeks, such as Copenhagen Fashion Week and Helsinki Fashion Week, have set a new standard for the industry. These events prioritize sustainability by featuring designers who use eco-friendly materials, ethical production methods, and innovative waste reduction techniques. By spotlighting sustainable fashion, these events encourage both designers and consumers to embrace more responsible practices.

Zero-waste fashion shows are another exciting development in the sustainable fashion movement. These events challenge designers to create collections with minimal waste, using techniques like upcycling, repurposing, and modular design. By pushing the boundaries of creativity, zero-waste fashion shows demonstrate the potential for a circular fashion economy and inspire a more sustainable approach to design.

Educational workshops and panels are also integral to sustainable fashion events. These sessions provide valuable insights into sustainable practices, ethical production, and responsible consumption. By fostering dialogue and knowledge-sharing, sustainable fashion events empower attendees to make informed choices and contribute to a more ethical industry. This chapter concludes by celebrating the impact of sustainable fashion events and their role in driving positive change.

10

Chapter 10: The Role of Technology in Sustainable Fashion

Technology is playing a pivotal role in transforming the fashion industry towards sustainability. This chapter explores the various technological advancements that are driving change, from digital design tools to blockchain for supply chain transparency. By leveraging technology, we can create a more efficient, ethical, and environmentally friendly fashion ecosystem.

Digital design tools are revolutionizing the way fashion is created and produced. Virtual prototyping, 3D modeling, and digital pattern-making allow designers to experiment and refine their creations without wasting physical materials. This not only reduces waste but also streamlines the design process, enabling more sustainable and innovative fashion.

Blockchain technology is another game-changer for the fashion industry. By providing a transparent and immutable record of each step in the supply chain, blockchain ensures that materials and products are sourced and produced ethically. This chapter delves into the potential of blockchain for improving supply chain transparency, reducing counterfeit products, and promoting fair labor practices.

Tech-driven recycling solutions are also making waves in the fashion industry. Innovations like chemical recycling, which breaks down synthetic fibers into their raw materials, and mechanical recycling, which transforms old garments into new textiles, offer promising solutions for reducing textile waste. This chapter highlights the importance of investing in and supporting these technologies to create a more circular fashion economy.

The role of technology in sustainable fashion extends to consumer engagement as well. Apps and platforms that promote secondhand shopping, clothing rental, and wardrobe management are encouraging more responsible consumption habits. By leveraging these tools, consumers can make more informed and sustainable fashion choices. This chapter concludes by celebrating the transformative potential of technology in driving sustainability in fashion.

11

Chapter 11: The Intersection of Culture and Sustainability

Cultural influences play a significant role in shaping our fashion choices and consumption patterns. This chapter explores the intersection of culture and sustainability, from traditional craftsmanship to contemporary movements. By understanding the cultural context of sustainable fashion, we can appreciate the diverse approaches to eco-friendly practices and celebrate the rich tapestry of global fashion.

Traditional craftsmanship has long been a cornerstone of sustainable fashion. Artisans around the world have honed their skills over generations, creating beautiful, durable, and eco-friendly garments. This chapter highlights the importance of preserving and supporting traditional craftsmanship, from handwoven textiles in India to intricate embroidery in Mexico. By valuing and investing in these artisanal practices, we can promote sustainability and cultural heritage.

Contemporary movements, such as the slow fashion movement, are also driving change in the industry. Slow fashion encourages a more thoughtful and intentional approach to fashion, prioritizing quality, longevity, and ethical production. This chapter delves into the principles of slow fashion and its impact on consumer behavior, emphasizing the importance of mindfulness and intentionality in our fashion choices.

The intersection of culture and sustainability is also evident in the rise of fashion activism. Designers and brands are using fashion as a platform for social and environmental advocacy, raising awareness about pressing issues and inspiring change. This chapter profiles some of the key figures in fashion activism, from Stella McCartney's commitment to cruelty-free fashion to Vivienne Westwood's climate change campaigns.

By understanding the cultural context of sustainable fashion, we can appreciate the diverse approaches to eco-friendly practices and celebrate the rich tapestry of global fashion. This chapter concludes by emphasizing the importance of cultural sensitivity and inclusivity in the sustainable fashion movement.

12

Chapter 12: Fashion and Climate Change

The fashion industry has a significant impact on climate change, from the carbon emissions associated with production to the energy-intensive processes involved in manufacturing and transportation. This chapter explores the relationship between fashion and climate change, highlighting the urgent need for the industry to reduce its carbon footprint and adopt more sustainable practices.

One of the main contributors to the fashion industry's carbon emissions is the production of synthetic fibers, such as polyester, which is derived from petroleum. The extraction and processing of petroleum release large amounts of greenhouse gases into the atmosphere. This chapter examines the environmental impact of synthetic fibers and explores alternatives, such as recycled polyester and bio-based fibers, that can help reduce the industry's carbon footprint.

Energy consumption is another critical issue in the fashion industry. The production, dyeing, and finishing of textiles require significant amounts of energy, much of which comes from fossil fuels. This chapter highlights the importance of adopting renewable energy sources and energy-efficient technologies in the fashion industry. By transitioning to cleaner energy sources, the industry can significantly reduce its carbon emissions and contribute to global climate goals.

The fashion industry's transportation and distribution networks also contribute to its carbon footprint. The global nature of the fashion supply chain means that garments often travel long distances from production to retail. This chapter explores the environmental impact of transportation and logistics in the fashion industry and emphasizes the need for more localized and sustainable supply chains. By supporting local production and reducing the distance garments travel, the industry can minimize its environmental impact.

13

Chapter 13: Circular Fashion Economy

A circular fashion economy is an alternative to the traditional linear model of "take, make, dispose." It emphasizes the importance of designing out waste, keeping products and materials in use, and regenerating natural systems. This chapter delves into the principles of a circular fashion economy and explores the strategies and innovations that can help achieve it.

Designing for longevity is a key principle of the circular fashion economy. By creating durable, high-quality garments that can withstand the test of time, designers can reduce the need for frequent replacement and minimize waste. This chapter highlights the importance of timeless design, quality materials, and craftsmanship in creating long-lasting fashion. By prioritizing durability and repairability, the industry can promote a more sustainable and circular approach to fashion.

Another essential strategy in a circular fashion economy is recycling and upcycling. By transforming old garments and textiles into new products, the industry can reduce the demand for virgin materials and minimize waste. This chapter explores the various recycling and upcycling techniques, from mechanical recycling to chemical recycling, and highlights successful case studies of circular fashion initiatives.

Renting and sharing fashion is also gaining popularity as a sustainable alternative to traditional ownership. Clothing rental platforms and fashion libraries allow consumers to access a wide range of garments without the need to purchase new items. This chapter delves into the benefits of fashion rental and sharing, from reducing waste to promoting a culture of reuse. By embracing these models, consumers can enjoy variety and novelty while supporting a more sustainable fashion system.

14

Chapter 14: Fashion and Social Justice

The fashion industry has long been associated with issues of social justice, from exploitative labor practices to unequal representation. This chapter explores the intersection of fashion and social justice, highlighting the importance of fair labor practices, diversity, and inclusion in the industry. By addressing these issues, we can create a more ethical and equitable fashion system.

Fair labor practices are a cornerstone of social justice in fashion. Many garment workers, particularly in developing countries, are subjected to poor working conditions, long hours, and low wages. This chapter examines the importance of ensuring fair labor practices, from safe working environments to living wages. By supporting brands that prioritize ethical labor practices, consumers can contribute to a more just and humane fashion industry.

Diversity and inclusion are also critical issues in the fashion industry. Historically, fashion has often been exclusionary, with narrow standards of beauty and limited representation of marginalized communities. This chapter explores the importance of diversity and inclusion in fashion, from the runway to advertising campaigns. By celebrating diverse identities and promoting inclusive practices, the industry can become a more representative and empowering space.

Fashion activism plays a vital role in advancing social justice. Designers, brands, and consumers are using fashion as a platform for advocacy and change. This chapter profiles some of the key figures and movements in fashion activism, from labor rights campaigns to body positivity initiatives. By leveraging the power of fashion for social good, we can drive meaningful change and create a more equitable industry.

15

Chapter 15: The Future of Sustainable Fashion

The future of sustainable fashion is filled with potential and promise. This chapter explores the emerging trends and innovations that are shaping the future of the industry, from bio-based materials to circular design principles. By embracing these advancements, the fashion industry can move towards a more sustainable and responsible future.

Bio-based materials, such as mushroom leather and algae fibers, are revolutionizing the fashion industry. These innovative materials offer sustainable alternatives to traditional textiles, with lower environmental impacts and unique properties. This chapter delves into the potential of bio-based materials and highlights some of the pioneering research and development efforts in this field.

Circular design principles are also gaining traction as a way to create a more sustainable fashion system. By designing products with their entire lifecycle in mind, from production to disposal, designers can minimize waste and promote a circular economy. This chapter explores the various aspects of circular design, including modularity, disassembly, and recyclability. By incorporating these principles, the industry can create products that are more sustainable and resilient.

The role of technology in sustainable fashion will continue to grow in importance. From AI-driven design tools to blockchain for supply chain transparency, technological advancements are driving innovation and efficiency in the industry. This chapter highlights some of the key technological trends and their potential to transform the fashion industry towards sustainability.

The future of sustainable fashion also depends on the actions of consumers. By making informed and responsible choices, supporting ethical brands, and embracing sustainable practices, consumers can drive change in the industry. This chapter concludes by emphasizing the importance of collective action and the power of individual choices in creating a more sustainable and responsible fashion future.

16

Chapter 16: The Role of Education in Sustainable Fashion

Education plays a critical role in shaping the future of sustainable fashion. By raising awareness and providing the tools and knowledge needed to make informed choices, education can empower individuals and communities to drive positive change in the industry. This chapter explores the various ways education is being leveraged to promote sustainability in fashion, from formal programs to grassroots initiatives.

Formal education programs, such as fashion design courses and sustainability-focused degrees, are equipping the next generation of designers and industry professionals with the skills and knowledge needed to create more sustainable fashion. This chapter highlights some of the leading institutions and programs that are championing sustainability in fashion education. By integrating sustainability into the curriculum, these programs are fostering a new wave of eco-conscious designers and industry leaders.

Grassroots initiatives and community-based education are also playing a vital role in promoting sustainable fashion. Workshops, seminars, and online resources are providing accessible and practical knowledge to consumers and aspiring designers. This chapter profiles some of the impactful grassroots initiatives that are making a difference, from local sewing collectives to online platforms that offer tutorials and resources on sustainable fashion practices.

Consumer education is another essential aspect of promoting sustainable fashion. By providing information on the environmental and social impacts of fashion, consumers can make more informed choices and support ethical brands. This chapter explores the importance of transparency and consumer engagement in driving change. By raising awareness and encouraging mindful consumption, education can empower individuals to make a positive impact on the fashion industry.

17

Chapter 17: A Call to Action

The journey towards sustainable fashion is ongoing, and it requires the collective efforts of designers, brands, consumers, and policymakers. This chapter serves as a call to action, urging readers to embrace the principles of sustainability and ethical responsibility in their fashion choices. By taking meaningful steps towards a more sustainable fashion future, we can protect the planet and ensure a more just and equitable industry.

One of the most powerful ways individuals can contribute to sustainable fashion is by making conscious choices. This chapter provides practical tips for incorporating sustainability into everyday fashion decisions, from choosing eco-friendly materials to supporting ethical brands. By prioritizing quality over quantity and embracing a more minimalist mindset, consumers can reduce their environmental impact and promote a more sustainable fashion industry.

Advocacy and activism are also critical components of driving change in the fashion industry. This chapter encourages readers to use their voices and platforms to raise awareness about the importance of sustainable fashion. By supporting campaigns, signing petitions, and engaging in discussions about sustainability, individuals can contribute to a broader movement for change. Advocacy efforts can also influence policymakers to implement regulations and policies that support sustainable practices in the fashion industry.

Collaboration and innovation are key to achieving a sustainable fashion future. This chapter emphasizes the importance of collaboration between designers, brands, consumers, and other stakeholders in the industry. By working together and sharing knowledge and resources, we can drive innovation and create solutions to the challenges facing the fashion industry. This collaborative approach can lead to the development of new materials, technologies, and business models that prioritize sustainability and ethical responsibility.

The chapter concludes by reiterating the importance of collective action and the power of individual choices in creating a more sustainable and responsible fashion future. By embracing the principles of eco-chic fashion and making informed choices, we can protect the planet, support ethical practices, and celebrate the intersection of style, sustainability, and moral responsibility.

In a world where fashion is both a means of self-expression and a major environmental culprit, **Eco-Chic: The Intersection of Style, Sustainability, and Moral Responsibility**" delves into the heart of the fashion paradox. This compelling narrative unveils the hidden costs of our clothing choices and offers a roadmap to a more ethical, sustainable, and stylish future.

Journey through the origins of fast fashion and explore the environmental and social consequences that have shaped the industry. Discover the innovative materials and technologies that are paving the way for a greener fashion landscape. From vintage treasures to the rise of ethical fashion brands, this book celebrates the creative solutions that are transforming the way we think about fashion.

Each chapter of "Eco-Chic" is a call to action, inviting readers to embrace responsible consumption, support fair labor practices, and champion diversity and inclusion in the fashion world. Through the lens of education, technology, and cultural influences, the book provides practical tips and inspiring stories that empower readers to make a positive impact.

Whether you're a fashion enthusiast, a sustainability advocate, or simply curious about the future of fashion, "Eco-Chic" is an essential guide to navigating the intersection of style, sustainability, and moral responsibility. Together, we can redefine fashion and create a world where looking good and doing good go hand in hand.

www.ingramcontent.com/pod-product-compliance
Lightning Source LLC
LaVergne TN
LVHW020457080526
838202LV00057B/6011